BOOK ONE

78 SELECTED DUETS

FOR TWO TRUMPETS
(Or Cornets)

(Easy – Intermediate)

Compiled and Edited by

JAY ARNOLD

This book presents the works of four masters of composition specifically for Trumpet or Cornet. These duets will appeal to the early grade players and will help advance them to the intermediate stage. Each player will, of course, master the selected part in solo form before associating the performance with the other part.

CONTENTS

THIRTY-NINE DUETS

WILHELM WURM

6

11 Andantino

16 Maestoso

17 Allegro

18 Andantino

20 Moderato

21 Allegretto

Andante

30

Moderato

31

20

Allegretto

37

38

Allegretto

39

SEVENTEEN DUETS

CARNAUD

RONDO
Allegro (♩=60 to ♩=104.)

MARCH TRIUMPHAL
Allo maestoso (♩=60 to ♩=76.)

15 Moderato (♩=92.)

FOURTEEN DUETS

DOMENICO GATTI

Andante tranquillo

Maestoso

Andantino

8

Andante moderato

12

molto espressivo

Allegro non troppo

EIGHT DUETS

SAINT-JACOME

Tempo I

MINUETTO
Vivace

TRIO
Sostenuto

D.S. %
to Minuetto with no repeats

Allegro moderato

Poco Adagio

Allegro leggiero